Microsoft Excel Formulas & Functions

A Practical Approach to Data Management

James Scottie

Copyright

Printed in the United States of America

©2024 by James Scottie

Table of Contents

Copyright ii

Why This Guide vii

About the Author.. viii

Introduction to excel.......................................1

Practical Applications of Excel.........................3

Notable Aspects of Excel Functions 4

Key Concepts in Excel Formulas 7

Components of Excel Function 8

Practical Application of Excel Function.........11

Basic Excel Functions and Formulas 11

SUM Functions 12

Count Functions 30

Logical Functions 34

Text Functions 43

Operator precedence 48

Introduction to Array Formulas 51

Array Constants 54

Lookup and Reference Functions 56

VLOOKUP Function...57

HLOOKUP Function 62

INDEX and MATCH Functions...................................66

Advantages of INDEX and MATCH over VLOOKUP 74

Two-way VLOOKUP Function.....................................74

References in Excel...78

Mathematical and Statistical Functions 79

Mathematical Functions...80

Statistical Functions 81

Date Function in Excel...82

Dynamic Creation of Date in Excel 86

ISBLANK Function Explained 92

Selected Practical Examples..94

Excel Tips, Tricks and Best Practices..........................105

Navigation and Selections 108

Excel Functions Quick Reference Guide....................111

Why This Guide

Are you an Excel novice looking to grasp the fundamentals or a seasoned professional aiming to harness the potency of Excel's formulas and functions for diverse data-oriented endeavors? This book is meticulously designed to cater to both audiences, addressing the inherent challenges encountered when navigating and employing Excel's functions and formulas proficiently. It's tailored to offer comprehensive guidance, tackling hurdles commonly faced while utilizing Excel's powerful tools for efficient data handling and analysis.

About the Author

James Scottie, an individual deeply passionate about technology, boasts a decade of involvement in the ICT sector. His fervor extends towards staying updated with the most recent advancements and trends in the technical domain. Educated at MIT in Boston, Massachusetts, he earned both a Bachelor's and a Master's Degree, majoring in Computer Science and Information Communication Technology James Scottie is a tech enthusiast with about 10 years' experience in the ICT industry.

Introduction to excel

Microsoft Excel is a robust and widely-used spreadsheet software developed by Microsoft. Renowned for its versatility and functionality, Excel is a part of the Microsoft Office suite and is designed to aid users in various tasks related to data management, analysis, and visualization.

It is a remarkably adaptable and widely employed tool in the Office suite. Regardless of your career path, expertise in Excel is crucial for achieving daily professional goals. Nevertheless, mastering the comprehensive functions and formulas within Excel is imperative for individuals to excel in their respective careers.

Key Components and Features:

1. **Grid-based Interface:** Excel operates on a grid system of rows and columns, forming cells where users can input data, formulas, or functions. This grid structure enables systematic organization and manipulation of data.

2. **Formulas and Functions:** Excel's strength lies in its ability to perform various calculations. Users

can create complex calculations using formulas and functions, enabling tasks such as basic arithmetic, statistical analysis, financial calculations, and logical operations.

3. **Data Analysis Tools:** Excel offers an array of tools for data analysis and manipulation. These tools include sorting, filtering, pivot tables, data validation, conditional formatting, and a wide range of built-in functions catering to diverse data analysis needs.

4. **Visual Representation with Charts:** Excel facilitates the creation of visual representations of data through charts and graphs. Users can choose from different chart types such as bar graphs, line charts, pie charts, and scatter plots to effectively communicate data trends and insights.

5. **Data Import and Export:** Excel allows users to import data from various sources such as databases, web queries, text files, and external systems. It also supports exporting data to

different formats, promoting interoperability with other software and systems.

6. **Customization and Formatting:** Users can customize Excel spreadsheets by formatting cells, applying styles, setting up conditional formatting rules, creating templates, and automating tasks through macros, enhancing productivity and visual appeal.

Practical Applications of Excel

1. **Business and Finance:** Excel is extensively used for financial modeling, budgeting, forecasting, accounting, and generating financial reports.

2. **Data Analysis and Reporting:** It serves as a powerful tool for analyzing datasets, generating reports, conducting statistical analysis, and visualizing trends.

3. **Project Management:** Excel aids in project planning, scheduling, resource management, and progress tracking through Gantt charts and project timelines.

4. **Educational and Personal Use:** Students, educators, and individuals utilize Excel for academic

purposes, calculations, organizing data, creating study materials, and managing personal finances.

Understanding Excel Functions

Excel functions are built-in tools that allow users to perform various calculations, manipulations, and analyses within spreadsheets. These functions are powerful and versatile, catering to a wide range of tasks, from simple arithmetic operations to complex data analysis.

Notable Aspects of Excel Functions

1. **Syntax and Arguments:** Each Excel function has a specific syntax and requires certain arguments or parameters to perform calculations. Understanding the syntax and how to correctly input arguments is crucial for using functions effectively.

2. **Categories of Functions:** Excel functions are categorized into different groups based on their functionalities:

- **Mathematical and Trigonometric Functions:** Perform basic arithmetic operatio trigonometric calculations, rounding, etc.

- **Statistical Functions:** Calculate statistical measures like mean, median, standard deviation, etc.

- **Logical Functions:** Assess conditions and return logical results (e.g., IF, AND, OR).

- **Lookup and Reference Functions:** Search for specific values within a dataset (e.g., VLOOKUP, HLOOKUP, INDEX, MATCH)

  - **Text Functions:** Manipulate and analyze text strings (e.g., CONCATENATE, LEFT, RIGHT).

  - **Date and Time Functions:** Handle date and time-related calculations and formatting.

3. **Nested Functions and Formulas:** Excel allows users to combine multiple functions within a single formula, known as nested functions. This technique enables users to perform more

intricate calculations by nesting functions inside one another.

4. **Dynamic and Volatile Functions:** Some functions in Excel are dynamic, recalculating whenever a change occurs in the worksheet (e.g., TODAY, NOW). Others, known as volatile functions, recalculate each time any change is made to the workbook (e.g., RAND, OFFSET).

5. **Error Handling:** Excel functions may return errors if used incorrectly or if the provided data is invalid. Understanding how to handle these errors using functions like IFERROR or IFNA is essential for maintaining accuracy in calculations.

Basics of Excel Formulas Excel formulas are expressions used to perform calculations, manipulate data, and automate tasks within spreadsheets. Understanding the basics of Excel formulas is fundamental for effective data management and analysis.

Key Concepts in Excel Formulas

1. **Syntax and Structure:** Formulas in Excel begin with an equal sign (=) followed by the function name and its arguments. The syntax must adhere to Excel's rules for correct execution.

2. **Operators:** Excel uses arithmetic operators (+, -, *, /), comparison operators (=, <>, >, <, >=, <=), and logical operators (AND, OR) within formulas to perform calculations and evaluations.

3. **References and Cell Addressing:** Formulas often reference cells, ranges, or named ranges. Cell references can be absolute (e.g., $A$1), relative (e.g., A1), or mixed (e.g., $A1 or A$1), impacting how the formula behaves when copied or moved.

4. **Functions:** Excel provides a wide range of built-in functions categorized into different groups (e.g., mathematical, statistical, logical, text). Functions perform specific operations and can be nested or combined within formulas for complex calculations.

5. **Basic Formulas and Functions:**

- **Arithmetic Operations:** Perform basic calculations like addition (+), subtraction (-), multiplication (*), division (/).

- **SUM Function:** Adds a range of numbers together (e.g., =SUM(A1:A10)).

- **AVERAGE Function:** Calculates the average of a range of values (e.g., =AVERAGE(B1:B20)).

- **IF Function:** Evaluates a condition and returns one value if true and another if false (e.g., =IF(C2>10, "Yes", "No")).

- **VLOOKUP Function:** Searches for a value in the first column of a table and returns a value in the same row from another column (e.g., =VLOOKUP(D2, A:B, 2, FALSE)).

Components of Excel Function

Components of Excel Functions: Arguments, Syntax, etc. Excel functions consist of various components that define their structure, execution, and output. Understanding these components—such as arguments, syntax, and function categories—is crucial for effectively utilizing Excel functions.

Key Components of Excel Functions:

1. **Syntax:** Every Excel function follows a specific syntax—a predefined structure that governs how the function is written. The syntax dictates the order of elements within the function, such as function name, parentheses, and arguments.

2. **Function Name:** Each function has a unique name that describes the operation it performs. Examples include SUM, AVERAGE, IF, VLOOKUP, and many more. Function names are used at the start of a formula to indicate which operation Excel should perform.

3. **Arguments:** Arguments are the inputs or parameters required by functions to perform calculations or actions. Functions can have multiple arguments, and each argument has a specific purpose. Arguments can be constants, cell references, ranges, or other functions.

4. **Argument Syntax:** Functions require specific types of arguments, such as numbers, text, logical values, cell references, or ranges. Understanding

the required argument syntax is essential for accurate function execution.

5. **Function Categories:** Excel functions are categorized into groups based on their functionalities, such as:

- **Mathematical and Trigonometric Functions:** Perform arithmetic and trigonometric operations.

- **Statistical Functions:** Calculate statistical measures (e.g., mean, median, standard deviation).

- **Logical Functions:** Evaluate logical conditions and return true/false values.

- **Lookup and Reference Functions:** Search and retrieve values from datasets.

- **Text Functions:** Manipulate and analyze text strings.

- **Date and Time Functions:** Handle date and time-related calculations and formatting.

6. **Function Arguments:**

- **Required Arguments:** Necessary inputs for a function to work correctly.

- **Optional Arguments:** Not always mandatory; functions can work without these inputs.

- **Default Arguments:** Some functions have default values for arguments if not explicitly specified.

Practical Application of Excel Function

Understanding function components enables users to:

- Write accurate and error-free formulas by correctly utilizing function names, syntax, and arguments.

- Perform diverse calculations, data manipulations, and analyses tailored to specific needs.

- Choose the appropriate functions for different data-related tasks, increasing efficiency in spreadsheet operations

Basic Excel Functions and Formulas

Basic Excel functions and formulas serve as fundamental tools for data manipulation, calculation, and analysis within spreadsheets. They empower users to perform various tasks, from simple calculations to complex data processing. These functions are the building blocks for creating powerful spreadsheets and are essential for anyone working with data in Excel.

SUM Functions

SUM Function: The SUM function in Excel is one of the most commonly used functions and is used to add numbers together. It allows users to quickly calculate the total of a range of cells or values.

Syntax:

```
=SUM(number 1, [number 2],...)
```

Parameters:

- **number1, number2, ... :** These are the numbers or cell references that you want to add together. You can input up to 255 numbers or cell references in the function separated by commas.

How to Use SUM Function:

1. **Basic Usage:**

- To sum a range of cells, select the cell where you want the total to appear.
- Type **=SUM(** and select the range of cells you want to add together. For example, **=SUM(A1:A10)** will add the values in cells A1 through A10.
- Press Enter to get the total sum.

Scenario

Suppose we want to find the sum from B2 to B3 as shown below.

	A	B	C	D	E
1	CLASS	Number of students			
2	A	20			
3	B	15	=SUM(B2:B3)		
4	C	10			
5	D	30			
6					
7					

2. **Adding Individual Values:**

- You can also directly input individual values separated by commas inside the SUM function. For example, **=SUM(5, 10, 15)** will give you the total sum of 5 + 10 + 15.

3. **Using Cell References:**

- Instead of typing the numbers directly, you can reference cell addresses. For instance, **=SUM(A1, B2, C3)** will add the values in cells A1, B2, and C3.

4. **Ranges with Non-Adjacent Cells:**

- You can select non-adjacent ranges or cells by separating them with commas inside the SUM function. For instance, **=SUM(B2:B5, C3:C7)** will add the values from cells B2 to B5 and C3 to C7 as displayed below.

	A	B	C	D	E	F
1			Month			
2	Name	Jan	Feb	Mar	Apr	
3	Brad	36	47	55	63	
4	Dave	42	58	65	72	
5	Cole	66	57	39	46	
6	Joseph	69	70	75	64	
7	Boby	45	48	51	58	
8						
9		=SUM(B3:B5,C3:C7)				
10						

- Then, press "Enter"

▲	A	B	C	D	E	F
1			Month			
2	Name	Jan	Feb	Mar	Apr	
3	Brad	36	47	55	63	
4	Dave	42	58	65	72	
5	Cole	66	57	39	46	
6	Joseph	69	70	75	64	
7	Boby	45	48	51	58	
8						
9		424				
10						
11						
12		==SUM(36,42,66,47,58,57,70,48)				
13						

SUMIF Function: The SUMIF function in Excel allows you to add up values in a range that meet specific criteria. It is particularly useful when you want to sum values based on certain conditions or criteria within a range.

=SUMIF(range, criteria,[sum_range])

Parameters:

- **range:** The range of cells that you want to evaluate based on the criteria.

- **criteria:** The condition or criteria used to determine which cells to add. It can be a number, expression, cell reference, or text that defines which cells will be added.

- **sum_range (optional):** The actual cells to be added if they meet the given criteria. If omitted, Excel will use the range parameter for summation (cells in range that meet the criteria).

How to Use SUMIF Function:

1. **Basic Usage:**

- To sum values based on a single condition, select the cell where you want the total to appear.

- Type =**SUMIF(** and input the range where the criteria will be applied, followed by the criteria itself.

Scenario

Suppose we want to get the total sales for 'Jan' in the table below.

=**SUMIF(A2:B6, B8,B2:B6)** will sum values in cells B2 through B6 where month is "Jan".

	A	B	C	D
1	Month	Sales		
2	Jan	$250		
3	Feb	$400		
4	Jan	$550		
5	Apr	$200		
6	May	$300		
7				
8	Month	Jan		
9	Sales	=SUMIF(A2:B6,B8,B2:B6)		
10				

- Press Enter to get the total sales for "Jan".

	A	B	C	D
1	Month	Sales		
2	Jan	$250		
3	Feb	$400		
4	Jan	$550		
5	Apr	$200		
6	May	$300		
7				
8	Month	Jan		
9	Sales	800		
10				

2. **Using Criteria with Cell Reference:**

- You can reference a cell that contains the criteria instead of directly typing it into the formula. For instance, **=SUMIF(A1:A10, B1)** will sum values in cells A1 through A10 that match the value in cell B1.

3. **Specifying a Separate Sum Range:**

- If you want to sum values from a different range than the evaluated range, include the sum_range parameter.

Another example, **=SUMIF(B2:B6, ">5", C2:C6)** will sum values in cells C2 through C6 corresponding to the cells in B2 through B6 that are greater than 5. To calculate the total amount of items sold exceeding 5 units, input the formula demonstrated above into an empty cell in excel sheet as shown below.

B8		▼	⋮	✕	✓	*fx*		=SUM

	A	B	C	D
1	Item	Unit Sold	amount	
2	Grocery	6	$200	
3	Bread	10	$450	
4	Orange	2	$70	
5	Drinks	5	$300	
6	Ice cream	15	$50	
7				
8		=SUMIF(B2:B6,">5",C2:C6)		
9				

Then, click "Enter"

| L14 | | ▾ | ⋮ | ✕ | ✓ | *fx* | |

▲	A	B	C	D	E
1	Item	Unit Sold	amount		
2	Grocery	6	$200		
3	Bread	10	$450		
4	Orange	2	$70		
5	Drinks	5	$300		
6	Ice cream	15	$50		
7					
8			700		
9					

SUMIFS Function: This function provides a powerful way to perform conditional summation based on multiple criteria, allowing users to analyze and sum data that meets multiple conditions simultaneously within specified ranges.

Syntax:

```
=SUMIFS(sum_range, criteria_range1, criteria1,
[criteria_range2, criteria2], ...)
```

Parameters:

- **sum_range:** The range of cells to be added when the specified criteria are met.

- **criteria_range1:** The range of cells to be evaluated based on the first criterion.

- **criteria1:** The condition or criteria used for the first range.

- **[criteria_range2, criteria2, ...]:** Additional ranges and criteria pairs can be added to refine the conditions for summation.

How to Use SUMIFS Function:

1. **Basic Usage with Single Criterion:**

- To sum values based on a single criterion, select the cell where you want the total to appear.
- Type **=SUMIFS(** and input the range to be summed, followed by the first criteria_range1, and criteria1. For example, **=SUMIFS(A2:A10, B2:B10, ">5")** will sum values in cells A2 through A10 where the corresponding cells in B2 through B10 are greater than 5.
- Press Enter to get the total sum.

2. **Adding Multiple Criteria:**

You can add additional pairs of criteria range and criteria to further refine the conditions for summation. For instance, **=SUMIFS(A2:A10, B2:B10, ">5", C2:C10, "<10")** will sum values in cells A2 through A10 where cells in B2 through B10 are greater than 5 and cells in C2 through C10 are less than 10.

Scenario

Suppose we want to find the total amount generated in the table below when the item is "Grocery" and the unit sold is greater than 10.

	A	B	C	D
1	Item	Unit Sold	amount	
2	Grocery	6	$200	
3	Bread	10	$450	
4	Orange	2	$70	
5	Drinks	5	$300	
6	Ice cream	15	$50	
7	Grocery	20	$150	
8	Bread	25	$220	
9	Drinks	10	$100	
10	Orange	25	$150	
11	Grocery	30	$300	
12				
13				

Step 1: Enter the formula containing the two conditions in a cell.

	A	B	C	D	E	F
1	Item	Unit Sold	amount			
2	Grocery	6	$200			
3	Bread	10	$450			
4	Orange	2	$70			
5	Drinks	5	$300			
6	Ice cream	15	$50			
7	Grocery	20	$150			
8	Bread	25	$220			
9	Drinks	10	$100			
10	Orange	25	$150			
11	Grocery	30	$300			
12						
13						
14		=SUMIFS(C2:C11,A2:A11,"Grocery",B2:B11,">5")				
15						

Then click "Enter"

	A	B	C	D	E
1	Item	Unit Sold	amount		
2	Grocery	6	$200		
3	Bread	10	$450		
4	Orange	2	$70		
5	Drinks	5	$300		
6	Ice cream	15	$50		
7	Grocery	20	$150		
8	Bread	25	$220		
9	Drinks	10	$100		
10	Orange	25	$150		
11	Grocery	30	$300		
12					
13					
14		450			

AVERAGE Function: The AVERAGE function is used to calculate the average (arithmetic mean) of a range of numbers. It allows you to find the average value of a

25

group of specified numbers. Here's how you can use the AVERAGE function with examples:

Syntax:

```
=AVERAG E(number1, [number2], ...)
```

number1, **number2**, etc.: These are the numeric values or cell references containing the numbers you want to average. You can include up to 255 arguments in the function.

To find the average of the total sales in the example below, simply enter the formula:

=AVERAGE(D2,D3,D4,D5)

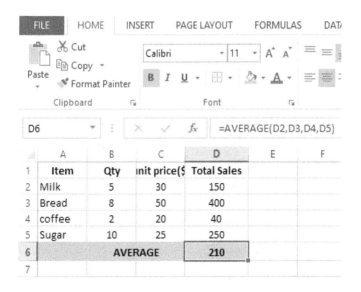

Alternatively, select the cells which you want to find their average

=AVERAGE(D2:D5)

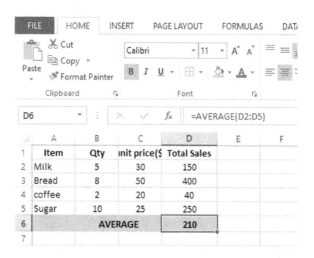

MAX Function: Finds the maximum value within a range of numbers.

Syntax:

```
=MAX(number1, [number2],...)

OR

=MAX(cell_range)
```

To find the maximum sale from the previous example, enter the formula in a cell as shown below.

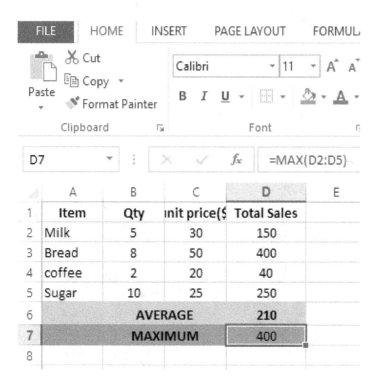

MIN Function: Finds the minimum value within a range of numbers.
Syntax:

```
=MIN(number1,[number2],...)

                    OR

=MIN(cell_range)
```

Count Functions

There are many count functions Excel each with distinctive purposes. Among them are:

COUNT: The COUNT function counts the number of cells within a range that contain numbers.

Syntax:

```
=COUNT(value1, [value2], ...)
```

Example

=COUNT(A1:A10)   // Counts the number of numeric

values in cells A1 to A10.

COUNTA: The COUNTA function counts the number of non-empty cells within a range containing any type of data (numbers, text, errors, logical values, etc.).

Syntax:

```
=COUNTA(value1, [value2], ...)
```

Example:

=COUNTA(A1:A10)   // Counts the number of non-blank cells in cells A1 to A10.

COUNTIF: The COUNTIF function counts the number of cells that meet a specific condition or criteria.

Syntax:

```
=COUNTIF(range, criteria)
```

=COUNTIF(A1:A10, ">5")   // Counts the number of values greater than 5 in cells A1 to A10.

Example

COUNTIFS: The COUNTIFS function counts the number of cells that meet multiple criteria across different ranges.

Syntax:

```
=COUNTIFS(criteria_range1, criteria1, [criteria_range2, criteria2], ...)
```

Scenario

Suppose we want to count the values greater than 10 in A2 to A11 and less than 20 in B2 to B11 in table below.

	A	B	C
1	**Entry A**	**Entry B**	
2	6	10	
3	10	20	
4	2	50	
5	5	25	
6	15	5	
7	20	15	
8	25	40	
9	10	25	
10	25	15	
11	30	20	
12			

Step 1: Enter "=COUNTIF()" in an empty cell

Step 2: Inside the parenthesis, select the first criteria range "A2:A11"

	A	B	C	D
1	Entry A	Entry B		
2	6	10		
3	10	20		
4	2	50		
5	5	25		
6	15	5		
7	20	15		
8	25	40		
9	10	25		
10	25	15		
11	30	20		
12				
13	=COUNTIFS(A2:A11			
14	COUNTIFS(**criteria_range1**, criteria1, ...)			

Step 3: Add comma and enter the first criterion ">10"

Step 4: Select the second criteria range, add a comma, and enter the second criterion.

	A	B	C	D
1	Entry A	Entry B		
2	6	10		
3	10	20		
4	2	50		
5	5	25		
6	15	5		
7	20	15		
8	25	40		
9	10	25		
10	25	15		
11	30	20		
12				
13	=COUNTIFS(A2:A11,">10",B2:B11,"<20")			
14				

Step 5: Press "Enter"

	A	B	C	D
1	Entry A	Entry B		
2	6	10		
3	10	20		
4	2	50		
5	5	25		
6	15	5		
7	20	15		
8	25	40		
9	10	25		
10	25	15		
11	30	20		
12				
13	3			
14				

COUNTBLANK: The COUNTBLANK function counts the number of empty cells within a specified range.

Syntax:

=COUNTBLANK(range)

Example

=COUNTBLANK(A1:A10)   // Counts the number of empty cells in cells A1 to A10.

Logical Functions

In Excel, logical functions are used to perform operations

34

based on logical conditions. These functions help in making decisions by evaluating conditions and returning true or false values. Some commonly used logical functions in Excel are analyzed in the table below. These functions help in creating complex logical operations and conditional statements within Excel spreadsheets, enabling users to perform calculations based on specific criteria or conditions. Here are some commonly used statistical functions in Excel.

IF Function: The IF function evaluates a condition and returns one value if the condition is true and another value if the condition is false.

Syntax:

```
=IF(logical_test, [value_if_true], [value_if_false])
```

Consider the table below, suppose we want to add remark such that if amount is greater than $1000, indicate "Over budget" else indicate "Normal".

	A	B	C
1	**Month**	**Budget**	
2	January	$10,000	
3	February	$20,000	
4	March	$5,000	
5	April	$55,000	
6	May	$15,000	
7	June	$3,000	
8			

To achieve our aim, enter the formula below in cell C2 and press "Enter"

=IF(B2 > 10000, "Over Budget", "Normal")

	A	B	C
1	**Month**	**Budget**	Remark
2	January	$10,000	Normal
3	February	$20,000	
4	March	$5,000	
5	April	$55,000	
6	May	$15,000	
7	June	$3,000	
8			

Drag cell C2 down to get remark for other values

	A	B	C	D
1	Month	Budget	Remark	
2	January	$10,000	Normal	
3	February	$20,000	Over Budget	
4	March	$5,000	Normal	
5	April	$55,000	Over Budget	
6	May	$15,000	Over Budget	
7	June	$3,000	Normal	
8				

AND Function: Checks if all the conditions specified are true and returns TRUE if they are, otherwise returns FALSE.

Syntax:

=AND(condition 1, condition 2, ...)

Condition 1 (required argument) – This is the first condition or logical value to be evaluated.

Condition 2 (optional requirement) – This is the second condition or logical value to be evaluated.

Note: The number of argument for AND can be up to 255

Scenario

If we aim to determine the bonus for each employee in our company at a rate of 5%, the criterion for eligibility includes a minimum tenure of five years in the industry, along with a sales equal to or exceeding $5000., and given the data below

	A	B	C	D	E	F	G	H
1			AND Function					
2	Name	Salary	Year	Sales	Bonus			
3	Dave	$50,000	10	$45,000	=IF(AND(C3>=5,D3>10000),B3*5%,0)			
4	William	$10,500	5	$70,000				
5	Joy	$7,000	3	$12,000				
6	Robot	$11,000	7	$5,000				
7	John	$12,000	2	$8,000				
8								

Click "Enter" and drag cell value E3 down

	A	B	C	D	E	F
1			AND Function			
2	Name	Salary	Year	Sales	Bonus	
3	Dave	$50,000	10	$45,000	2500	
4	William	$10,500	5	$70,000	525	
5	Joy	$7,000	3	$12,000	0	
6	Robot	$11,000	7	$5,000	0	
7	John	$12,000	2	$8,000	0	
8						

OR Function: Checks if at least one condition is true and returns TRUE if any condition is true; otherwise, returns FALSE

Syntax:

=OR(condition 1, condition 2, ...)

In the given situation, an employee's qualification for receiving a 5% bonus relies on the discretion of the management, based on either possessing a minimum of five years' experience or achieving sales totaling at least $5000.

Hence, the utilization of the OR function in this instance is pertinent, as illustrated below.

	A	B	C	D	E	F	G
1			AND Function				
2	Name	Salary	Year	Sales	Bonus		
3	Dave	$50,000	10	$45,000	=IF(OR(C3>=5,D3>=5),B3*5%,0)		
4	William	$10,500	5	$70,000			
5	Joy	$7,000	3	$12,000			
6	Robot	$11,000	7	$5,000			
7	John	$12,000	2	$8,000			
8							

Then Press "Enter"

	A	B	C	D	E	F
1			AND Function			
2	Name	Salary	Year	Sales	Bonus	
3	Dave	$50,000	10	$45,000	2500	
4	William	$10,500	5	$70,000	525	
5	Joy	$7,000	3	$12,000	350	
6	Robot	$11,000	7	$5,000	550	
7	John	$12,000	2	$8,000	600	
8						

IFERROR: The IFERROR function in Excel is used to handle errors that may occur in formulas. It allows you to specify the value or action to be taken if an error is encountered in a formula, making your spreadsheets more robust and preventing error messages from appearing to the end-user.

The IFERROR function is handy when dealing with calculations that may encounter errors due to various reasons, such as division by zero, invalid data, or other mathematical operations resulting in errors (#DIV/0!, #VALUE!, #REF!, etc.).

Syntax:

=IFERROR(value, value_if_error)

value: This is the expression or formula that you want to evaluate.

value_if_error: This is the value or action to be taken if an error occurs while evaluating the value parameter.

For example, Excel returns divide by zero error(#DIV/O!) when a formula tries to divide a number by zero as shown below.

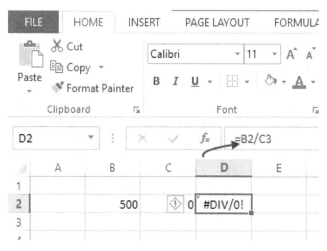

The IFFERROR is used to handle the error as shown below by inserting a specified value if error occurred.

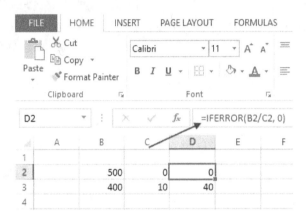

NOT Function: The Not Function reverses the logical value of its argument. If the argument is true, it returns false, and if the argument is false, it returns true.

Syntax:

=NOT(logical_expression)

Consider the example below, = (500 = 500) returns TRUE, while =NOT(500 = 500) returns FALSE

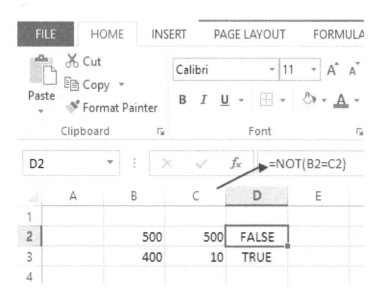

Text Functions

Excel offers various text functions to manipulate and work with text strings within cells. These text functions offer various ways to manipulate and work with text strings, allowing users to extract specific parts of text, modify case, combine or split text, find positions of characters, and perform various other text-related operations within spreadsheets. Some commonly used text functions include

CONCATENATE: The Concatenates (joins together) multiple strings into one.

Syntax:

```
=CONCATENATE(text1, [text2], ...)
```

Scenario

Suppose we want to concatenate First Name and Surname in the table below.

	A	B	C
1	**First Name**	**Last Name**	
2	Cole	Brale	
3	Grey	John	
4	Joshua	Clay	
5	James	Mary	
6	Jennifer	Anya	
7			

Step 1: Enter the formula in an empty cell, separate the names with space as shown below

44

	A	B	C	D	E
1	First Name	Last Name	Name		
2	Cole	Brale	=CONCATENATE(A2," ",B2)		
3	Grey	John			
4	Joshua	Clay			
5	James	Mary			
6	Jennifer	Anya			
7					

Then press "Enter" and draw down to fill the remaining cells.

	A	B	C
1	First Name	Last Name	Name
2	Cole	Brale	Cole Brale
3	Grey	John	Grey John
4	Joshua	Clay	Joshua Clay
5	James	Mary	James Mary
6	Jennifer	Anya	Jennifer Anya
7			

LEFT Function: This extracts a specified number of characters from the left side of a text string.

Syntax:

```
=LEFT(text, num_chars)
```

Suppose we want to extract every first 5 characters from each text string in table below.

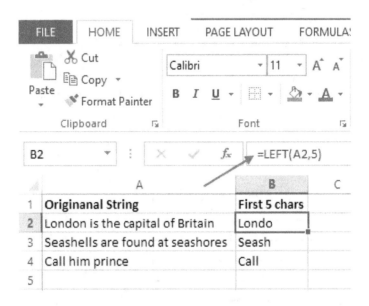

REPLACE Function: Replaces characters within a text string with new text.

Syntax:

Arguments:

old_text: This is the original text string where you want to perform the replacement.

start_num: It represents the starting position in the old_text where the replacement will begin.

num_chars: It indicates the number of characters in the old_text that will be replaced.

new_text: The text that will replace the specified segment in the old_text.

The example below is intended to replace "work" In "The work is 98% completion" with "Project".

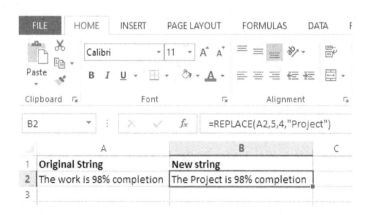

Explanation:

1. The first argument of the REPLACE function is A2, which contains the original string to be replaced.

2. The second argument is 5, which indicates the starting letter of the original string to be replaced

3. The third argument is 4, which is the number of characters to be replaced.

4. The fourth and last parameter is "Project", a new string to be replaced with.

The old string is "work", and the new string is "Project"

Operator precedence

Operator precedence determines the order in which mathematical operations are performed in a formula. Understanding operator precedence helps in correctly evaluating complex formulas.

Understanding operator precedence is crucial for constructing accurate formulas, especially in complex scenarios. However, mistakes with parentheses can lead to errors. Forgetting to close parentheses properly can result in Excel flagging an error. Excel might suggest closing the formula with a misplaced parenthesis, potentially leading to an incorrect result. Hence, knowing where to place closing parentheses is essential for accurate calculations

The following is the order of operator precedence in Excel, from highest to lowest:

Order	Operator	Remark
1	Parentheses ()	Operations inside parentheses are performed first. They can be used to explicitly define the order of operations.
2	Exponents (^)	Exponentiation operations are performed next.
3	Multiplication (*) and Division (/)	Multiplication and division have the same precedence and are evaluated from left to right.
4	Addition (+) and Subtraction (-)	Addition and subtraction also have the same precedence and are evaluated from left to right.
5	Concatenation (&)	The ampersand (&) operator for text concatenation is performed after arithmetic operations.

		These operators compare values and return TRUE or FALSE. Greater Than (>), Less Than (<), Greater Than or Equal To (>=), Less Than or Equal To (<=), Equal To (=), Not Equal To (<>).
6	Comparison Operators	
7	Logical Operators	Used for logical operations. AND, OR, NOT.

Illustration:

Using parentheses is crucial in Excel as it determines the order of calculations within a formula. By employing parentheses, you instruct Excel to prioritize specific operations. Note that multiplication, division, and comparison operators share the same precedence level. When operators have the same precedence, Excel processes them from left to right.

Consider the formula =10+8*2. Excel evaluates this as 26 because it prioritizes multiplication over addition. However, if we use parentheses like = (10+8)*2, Excel computes 10+8 first (resulting in 18) due to the parentheses, then multiplies this by 2, giving the result 36.

In more complex formulas with multiple sets of parentheses, Excel follows an "inside-out" approach. For instance, in the formula =5*(10-(2*3)/2):

1. Excel calculates (2*3) *first, resulting in 6. The formula then becomes =5*(10-6/2).*

2. Next, Excel computes 6/2 (yielding 3) due to the higher precedence of division over subtraction. The formula now reads =5*(10-3).

3. Finally, Excel calculates (10-3), resulting in 7, and then multiplies this by 5, leading to the final result of 35

Introduction to Array Formulas

An array formula is a powerful feature in excel that enables you to perform calculations on arrays of data rather than individual cells. It allows you to perform multiple calculations, comparisons, or other operations across a range of cells or multiple ranges. Array formulas enable simultaneous computation and manipulation of data, making them powerful tools for advanced   calculations, data analysis, and   complex calculations that involve multiple conditions.

Characteristics of array formulas

1. **Handling Multiple Cells/Values:** Array formulas can process entire arrays or ranges of data at once, performing calculations on multiple cells or data sets within a single formula.

2. **Syntax:** To create an array formula, you need to input the formula using a specific syntax. Instead of pressing Enter after typing the formula, you press Ctrl + Shift + Enter (for Windows) or Command + Enter (for Mac). Excel will automatically enclose the formula in curly braces {} to indicate that it's an array formula.

3. **Single Cell Output:** Although array formulas operate on multiple cells or ranges, they typically return a single value, which might spill into adjacent cells if the result is more than one cell.

4. **Ctrl + Shift + Enter:** To create an array formula, users often need to use Ctrl + Shift + Enter (CSE) instead of just pressing Enter. This

tells Excel that the formula is an array formula, and Excel encloses the formula in curly braces {} to signify this.

5. **Array Functions:** Excel provides specific functions designed to work with arrays, such as TRANSPOSE, MMULT, INDEX, MATCH, etc. These functions are meant to handle arrays efficiently.

6. **Performing Complex Operations:** Array formulas enable various complex operations like matrix calculations, multi-criteria calculations, conditional calculations, and more, often simplifying what would otherwise require multiple steps or separate formulas.

7. **Dynamic Array Formulas (Excel 365):** In Excel 365, dynamic array formulas were introduced, allowing certain functions to spill results automatically across multiple cells without requiring CSE. Functions like FILTER, SORT, UNIQUE, and SEQUENCE belong to this category.

8. **Memory and Performance:** Array formulas might consume more memory and could potentially slow down the spreadsheet, especially with large datasets or complex formulas. Efficient use of array formulas is crucial for maintaining good performance **Examples:**

✓ **SUM with Array Formula:** For example, to sum the values in range A1:A5, you can use an array formula like **{=SUM(A1:A10)}** entered with Ctrl + Shift + Enter.

✓ **Multiple Criteria with Array Formula:** To count the number of values greater than 50 and less than 100 in range B1:B10, you can use an array formula like **{=COUNTIF((B1:B10 > 50) * (B1:B10 < 100), TRUE)}**.

✓ **Matrix Operations:** You can perform matrix operations using array formulas with functions like MMULT for matrix multiplication, TRANSPOSE for transposing arrays, etc.

Array Constants

Array constants in Excel refer to constant values or data arranged in an array format within a formula.

They are used as direct inputs to formulas or array functions without referencing cells or ranges.

Array constants in Excel have specific syntax:

- Enclosed in curly braces {}.
- Elements within the array are separated by commas.
- Multiple rows are separated by semicolons (;).
  For example:
- A one-dimensional array constant: **{1, 2, 3, 4, 5}**
- A two-dimensional array constant: **{ {"Apple", "Orange", "Banana"}, {10, 20, 30}, {TRUE, FALSE, TRUE} }**

Array constants can be utilized in various ways within Excel formulas:

- **Direct Input in Formulas:** Array constants can be used directly within formulas to perform calculations or operations. For instance, you can use **{1, 2, 3, 4, 5}** in a formula to calculate the sum or average of these numbers without referencing specific cells.

1. **Array Functions:** Some functions in Excel, such as TRANSPOSE or MMULT, accept array constants as arguments. These functions perform operations on arrays, and array constants can be directly used within these functions to manipulate data.

2. **Custom Array Operations:** Array constants can be employed to create custom arrays for specific calculations or operations that require structured data in a formula.

Example:

=SUM({1, 2, 3, 4, 5}) - This formula calculates the sum of the numbers 1 to 5 without referencing cells.

Lookup and Reference Functions

Excel offers various lookup functions aiding users in locating particular information within cell ranges, tables, or arrays. This guide will introduce the frequently utilized lookup functions, notably VLOOKUP, HLOOKUP, as well as the INDEX and MATCH functions.

VLOOKUP Function

The VLOOKUP function in Excel stands for "Vertical Lookup." This function allows users to search for a value in the leftmost column of a table or range and retrieve a corresponding value from the same row in a specified column. It's commonly used to perform approximate or exact matches within a dataset.

Syntax:

```
=VLOOKUP(lookup_value, table array, col_index_num,
[range_lookup])
```

Components of the VLOOKUP Function

1. **lookup_value:** This is the value you want to find within the leftmost column of the table or range.

2. **table_array:** This refers to the table or range where you want to perform the lookup. It includes the column from which to retrieve the value based on the match found in the leftmost column.

3. **col_index_num:** It specifies the column number in the table_array from which the matching value should be returned. For instance, if you want to retrieve data from the third column of the table_array, col_index_num would be 3.

4. **range_lookup (optional):** This argument can be either TRUE (approximate match) or FALSE (exact match). If set to TRUE or omitted, VLOOKUP will search for an approximate match. If set to FALSE, it will look for an exact match. It's recommended to use FALSE for precise results.

How to use VLOOKUP Function

VLOOKUP is particularly useful in scenarios where you're seeking a corresponding data point in a column, and upon locating it, you retrieve a value positioned a specified number of columns to the right. Analogously, it's akin to the experience in high school when exam scores were posted on a notice board. Students eagerly scanned for their names or enrollment numbers. Once found, their gaze shifted to the right to obtain their scores. This analogy vividly illustrates the functionality of the VLOOKUP function in Excel.

For example, find John's Score in Physics, given the table below.

	A	B	C	D	E	F
1			Subject			
2	Name	English	Maths	Physics	Chemistry	
3	Brad	36	47	55	63	
4	Dave	42	58	65	72	
5	Cole	66	57	39	46	
6	Joseph	69	73	75	64	
7	Boby	45	48	51	58	
8						
9		Joseph				
10		=VLOOKUP(B9,A3:E7,4,0)				
11						

In the **Formula Bar**, type **=VLOOKUP()**.

1. In the parentheses, enter your lookup value, followed by a comma. This can be an actual value, or a blank cell that will hold a value: **(B9,**
2. Enter your table array or lookup table, the range of data you want to search, and a comma: **(B9,A3:E7,**

3. Enter column index number. This is the column where you think the answers are, and it must be to the right of your lookup values: **(B9,A3:E7,4,**

4. Enter the range lookup value, either **TRUE** or **FALSE**. TRUE finds partial matches, FALSE finds exact matches Your finished formula looks something like this: **=VLOOKUP(B9,A3:E7,4,FALSE)**

Then, click "Enter"

	A	B	C	D	E
1			Subject		
2	Name	English	Maths	Physics	Chemistry
3	Brad	36	47	55	63
4	Dave	42	58	65	72
5	Cole	66	57	39	46
6	Joseph	69	73	75	64
7	Boby	45	48	51	58
8					
9		Joseph			
10		75			
11					

Here is the formula that returns joseph Physics mark

=VLOOKUP("Joseph",$A$3:$E$7,4,0)

The above formula has four arguments:

- "Joseph: – this is the lookup value.
- $A$3:$E$7 – this is the range of cells in which we are looking. Remember that Excel looks for the lookup value in the left-most column. In this example, it would look for the name Joseph in A3:A7 (which is the left-most column of the specified array).
- 4 – Once the function spots Joseph's name, it will go to the second column of the array, and return the value in the same row as that of Joseph. The value 4 here indicated that we are looking for the score from the fourth column of the specified array.
- 0 – this tells the VLOOKUP function to only look for exact matches.

Key Considerations:

- Ensure that the leftmost column of the table_array contains the lookup values. VLOOKUP searches from left to right.

- The col_index_num specifies the column number (relative to the table_array) from which to retrieve the data.

- For the most accurate results, set range_lookup to FALSE to perform an exact match.

HLOOKUP Function

The HLOOKUP function in Excel stands for "Horizontal Lookup." It is a powerful tool used for searching and retrieving data from a table or range based on a specified criteria, similar to VLOOKUP. However, unlike VLOOKUP which searches vertically, HLOOKUP performs a horizontal lookup by scanning the top row of a table or range to locate a specified value and returns a corresponding value from the specified row.

Searches for a value in the first row of a table and returns a value in the same column from another row.

Syntax:

```
=HLOOKUP(lookup_value,table_array, row_index_num,
[range_lookup])
```

Arguments:

1. lookup_value: This is the value you want to find within the top row of the table or range.

2. table_array: This refers to the table or range where you want to perform the lookup. It includes the row from which to retrieve the value based on the match found in the top row.

3. row_index_num: It specifies the row number in the table_array from which the matching value should be returned. For example, if you want to retrieve data from the third row of the table_array, row_index_num would be 3.

4. range_lookup (optional): This argument can be either TRUE (approximate match) or FALSE (exact match), similar to VLOOKUP. If set to TRUE or omitted, HLOOKUP will search for an approximate match. If set to FALSE, it will look for an exact match.

Example

Consider the table below of students and their scores in each subject.

	A	B	C	D	E	F
1	Name	Student A	Student B	Student C	Student D	
2	English	75	65	82	55	
3	Maths	64	81	79	68	
4	Physics	92	76	49	98	
5	Chemistry	72	52	75	54	
6	Economics	54	83	68	60	
7						

Suppose our objective is to fetch the mark of Student D in Chemistry, we can use HLOOKUP Function as follows.

In an empty cell, type =HLOOKUP( )

Then, enter the lookup value by typing "Student D" or select the reference cell, B8 in this case.

	A	B	C	D	E	F
1	Name	Student A	Student B	Student C	Student D	
2	English	75	65	82	55	
3	Maths	64	81	79	68	
4	Physics	92	76	49	98	
5	Chemistry	72	52	75	54	
6	Economics	54	83	68	60	
7						
8		Student A				
9		=HLOOKUP(C13,				

64

Now, select the table_array

	A	B	C	D	E	F
1	Name	Student A	Student B	Student C	Student D	
2	English	75	65	82	55	
3	Maths	64	81	79	68	
4	Physics	92	76	49	98	
5	Chemistry	72	52	75	54	
6	Economics	54	83	68	60	
7						
8		Student A				
9		=HLOOKUP(C13,A1:E6,				

Then, enter the row number where the lookup value can be found.

	A	B	C	D	E
1	Name	Student A	Student B	Student C	Student D
2	English	75	65	82	55
3	Maths	64	81	79	68
4	Physics	92	76	49	98
5	Chemistry	72	52	75	54
6	Economics	54	83	68	60
7					
8		Student A			
9		=HLOOKUP(C13,A1:E6,4,			

Enter "0" or false for exact match

	A	B	C	D	E	F
1	Name	Student A	Student B	Student C	Student D	
2	English	75	65	82	55	
3	Maths	64	81	79	68	
4	Physics	92	76	49	98	
5	Chemistry	72	52	75	54	
6	Economics	54	83	68	60	
7						
8		Student A				
9		=HLOOKUP(C13,A1:E6,4,FALSE)				

Press "Enter" The result is 98

	A	B	C	D	E	F
1	Name	Student A	Student B	Student C	Student D	
2	English	75	65	82	55	
3	Maths	64	81	79	68	
4	Physics	92	76	49	98	
5	Chemistry	72	52	75	54	
6	Economics	54	83	68	60	
7						
8		Student D				
9	Physiscs	98				
10						

INDEX and MATCH Functions

The INDEX and MATCH functions in Excel are powerful tools used together for looking up and retrieving data within a table or range based on specific criteria.

INDEX Function Explained

INDEX function in Excel is used to retrieve data from a specific position within a table or range. It's a versatile function that allows you to fetch a value from a range based on row and column numbers, or based on a matching condition.

The basic syntax of the INDEX function is:

=INDEX(array, row_num, [column_num]) **array**: This is the range or array from which you want to retrieve data.

Arguments

- **row_num**: The row number within the array from which you want to fetch the data.

- **column_num** (optional): The column number within the array from which you want to fetch the data. This argument is required if the array is two-dimensional. If omitted, only the row number is used.

Common Use cases of INDEX Function

Here are a few common uses of the INDEX function:

1. **Single Dimension Array (One Column or Row):**

To fetch a value from a single column or row, for example, if you have values in cells A1 to A5 and you want to retrieve the value from the third cell:

=INDEX(A1:A5, 3)

2. Two-Dimensional Array (Table or Range):

If you have a table with data in cells A2 to C5 and you want to retrieve the value from the second row and third column:

Enter the formula =INDEX(A2:C5, 2, 3)

	A	B	C	D
	A7	▼ ⋮ ✕ ✓ fx	=INI	
	A	B	C	D
1	20	10	22	
2	10	15	12	
3	14	5	18	
4	12	40	31	
5	25	12	10	
6				
7	=INDEX(A1:C5,2,3)			

Then, click: "Enter"

	A	B	C	D
1	20	10	22	
2	10	15	12	
3	14	5	18	
4	12	40	31	
5	25	12	10	
6				
7	12			
8				

MATCH Function Explained

The MATCH function in Excel is used to find the position (row or column number) of a specified value within a range. It's useful for searching within a single row, single column, or an array, and it returns the relative position of the value within that range.

The basic syntax of the MATCH function:

```
=MATCH(lookup_value, lookup_array, [match_type])
```

Arguments

> **lookup_value**: The value you want to find within the **lookup_array**.

> **lookup_array**: The range or array where you want to search for the **lookup_value**.

> **match_type** (optional): It specifies the type of match:

- **0** (Exact match, or "FALSE") - Finds the exact match.

- **1** (Less than, or "TRUE") - Finds the largest value that is less than or equal to the **lookup_value**. The **lookup_array** should be sorted in ascending order.

- **-1** (Greater than, or "TRUE") - Finds the smallest value that is greater than or equal to the **lookup_value**. The **lookup_array** should be sorted in descending order.

Here are a few examples of using the MATCH function:

1. **Finding the Position of a Value in a Column:**

If you want to find the position of the value "Apple" in column A (A1 to A10):

=MATCH("Apple", A1:A10, 0)

2. Finding the Position of a Value in a Row:

If you have values in row 1 (A1 to J1) and you want to find the position of the value "XYZ":

=MATCH("XYZ", 1:1, 0)

3. Using Match Type:

If you're looking for an approximate match (less than or equal to) and you have values in column B (B1 to B10):

=MATCH(500, B1:B10, 1)

INDEX and MATCH Combination

Used together, INDEX and MATCH create a dynamic lookup formula that can search for a specific value and return a corresponding value from a different column or row. This combination allows for more flexible and powerful lookups by using the INDEX function to retrieve a value based on a row and column number and the

MATCH function to find the position of a value within a range.

```
=INDEX(return_range,MATCH(lookup_value, lookup_range, 0))
```

- return_range: The range from which to return the final value.
- lookup_value: The value to search for in the lookup_range.
- lookup_range: The range or array where the value is searched.

Scenario

Suppose you have a table with product names in column A and their corresponding prices in column B. You want to find the price of a specific product, say "Product X."

The formula would be:

=INDEX(B:B, MATCH("Product X", A:A, 0))

This formula searches for "Product X" in column A using MATCH. Once found, INDEX returns the corresponding value from column B, which is the price of "Product X". This is illustrated in the table below;

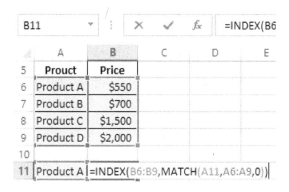

Then, click "Enter"

	A	B	C
5	**Prouct**	**Price**	
6	Product A	$550	
7	Product B	$700	
8	Product C	$1,500	
9	Product D	$2,000	
10			
11	Product A	550	
12			

J13 — Name Box

Advantages of INDEX and MATCH over VLOOKUP

➢ No Limitation on Lookup Columns: INDEX and MATCH can look up data from the leftmost column, unlike VLOOKUP, which requires the lookup value to be in the leftmost column.

➢ Dynamic Column Selection: With MATCH, you can dynamically choose the column number based on specific criteria.

➢ Handling Non-Exact Matches: MATCH offers more flexibility in handling non-exact matches by specifying match_type as 1 or -1.

Two-way VLOOKUP Function

The standard VLOOKUP function is designed to search for values in a column and retrieve corresponding values from the same row. However, when you need to find a value that matches both horizontally and vertically (like in a matrix or table), the traditional VLOOKUP alone might not suffice. This is where the two-way VLOOKUP technique becomes handy. The two-way VLOOKUP involves using two VLOOKUP functions in sequence to perform bidirectional searches within a table or dataset. It's a valuable technique when searching for data that lies across both rows and columns in Excel, allowing for more dynamic data retrieval.

Implementation of Two-Way VLOOKUP

1. **Horizontal VLOOKUP:**

- Use the regular VLOOKUP function to search for a value in the first row of the table. This will retrieve a reference number (column index number).
- The reference number will help in identifying the column where the desired data resides.

2. **Vertical VLOOKUP:**

- Utilize the reference number obtained from the horizontal VLOOKUP as the column index number for another VLOOKUP function.
- This VLOOKUP will search for the desired value in a specific column (identified by the reference number) and retrieve the result from a particular row.

Let's consider the previous table with students' data where column A contains student names, row 1 contains subjects and the cells contains scores figures.

Horizontal VLOOKUP: Search for the month (e.g., "Physics") in row 1 to obtain the column index number (let's say it's column 4).

Vertical VLOOKUP: Use the obtained column index number (4 in this case) as the column index number for another VLOOKUP.

Search for the student name (e.g., "John") in column A and retrieve the scores figure from the corresponding cell in column 4.

The Two-way lookup function will enable us to change either student name or subject and the VLOOKUP function. The implication of this is that we need to make the column dynamic as well. To do this, we need to use the MATCH Function as the column argument as indicated below.

=VLOOKUP(B10,$A$2:E,MATCH(C9,$A$2:$E$2,0),0)

Enter the formula stated above.

	A	B	C	D	E	F	G	H
1			Subject					
2	Name	English	Math	Physics	Chemistry			
3	Brad	36	47	55	63			
4	Dave	42	58	65	72			
5	Cole	66	57	39	46			
6	Joseph	69	70	75	64			
7	Boby	45	48	51	58			
8								
9			Chemistry					
10		Boby	=VLOOKUP(B10,$A$3:$E$7,MATCH(C9,$A$2:$E$2,0),0)					
11								

Then click "Enter'

	A	B	C	D	E	F
1			Subject			
2	Name	English	Math	Physics	Chemistry	
3	Brad	36	47	55	63	
4	Dave	42	58	65	72	
5	Cole	66	57	39	46	
6	Joseph	69	70	75	64	
7	Boby	45	48	51	58	
8						
9			Chemistry			
10		Boby	58			
11						

When you change student um and/subject in C9, a new score appears.

References in Excel

In Excel, references play a crucial role in formulas and functions. They indicate the location of cells or ranges within a worksheet and help Excel understand which data to use in calculations or lookups. References can be absolute, relative, or mixed:

Absolute Reference ($A$1): An absolute reference remains fixed when a formula is copied to other cells. It is denoted by the "$" symbol before both the column letter and row number, such as $A$1.

78

Relative Reference (A1): A relative reference changes when a formula is copied to other cells. It refers to a cell relative to the location of the formula. For example, if the formula is moved one cell down, the reference changes from A1 to A2.

Mixed Reference ($A1 or A$1): A mixed reference contains an absolute or relative component. "$A1" refers to an absolute column (column A) and a relative row (row 1), while "A$1" refers to a relative column and an absolute row.

Mathematical and Statistical Functions

Mathematical and statistical functions play a crucial role in performing various calculations, data analysis, and numerical operations. These functions enable users to perform various mathematical calculations, statistical analyses, and data manipulations within Excel, making it a versatile tool for handling numerical data in worksheets and workbooks.

Here's an overview of some commonly used mathematical and statistical functions:

Mathematical Functions

Excel offers a variety of mathematical functions for performing arithmetic operations, statistical calculations, rounding, and more. Here are some commonly used mathematical functions in Excel:

1. **SUM:** Adds up numbers in a range.

   =SUM(A2:A10) // Add value in cell A2 through cell A10

2. **AVERAGE:** Calculates the average of numbers in a range or selected cell references.

   =AVERAGE(B2:B20)

3. **MAX/MIN:** Returns the maximum/minimum value from a range of cells.

   =MAX(C2:C100)

4. **ROUND:** Rounds a number to a specified number of digits.

   =ROUND(D2, 2) (Rounds the value in cell D1 to 2 decimal

   places)

5. **ABS:** Returns the absolute value of a number.

   =ABS(E2)

6. **POWER:** Raises a number to a specified power. **=POWER(F1, G1)** (Raises the value in cell F1 to the power of the value in cell G1)

Statistical Functions

Excel provides a range of statistical functions that enable users to analyze data, calculate descriptive statistics, and perform various statistical operations. Here are some commonly used statistical functions in Excel:

1. **COUNT/COUNTA:** Counts the number of cells containing numbers/non-blank cells.

   =COUNT(H1:H50) or **=COUNTA(I1:I100)**

2. **COUNTIF/COUNTIFS:** Counts cells that meet specific criteria.

   =COUNTIF(J1:J200, ">50") (Counts cells in J1:J200 that are greater than 50)

3. **SUMIF/SUMIFS:** Adds cells based on a given criterion/criteria.

   =SUMIF(K1:K100, ">100", L1:L100) (Sums values in L1:L100 if the corresponding cells in K1:K100 are greater than 100)

4. **AVERAGEIF/AVERAGEIFS:** Calculates the average based on a given criterion/criteria.

   =AVERAGEIF(M1:M50, "<>0") (Calculates the average of
   non-zero values in M1:M50)

Date Function in Excel

The DATE function in Excel is a powerful tool used to create a date value by specifying the year, month, and day as separate arguments. It returns the serial number representing the specified date based on the provided year, month, and day values.

The syntax of the DATE function is as follows:

=DATE(year, month, day)

- **year**: Represents the year you want to use to create the date. It should be a four-digit number (e.g., 2023).

- **month**: Denotes the month you want to use to create the date. It should be a number between 1 (for January) and 12 (for December).

- **day**: Signifies the day you want to use to create the date. It should be a number between 1 and 31, depending on the month and year (e.g., 1 for the 1st day of the month).

The DATE function generates a serial number that corresponds to the specified date according to Excel's date system. In Excel, dates are stored as sequential serial numbers, with January 1, 1900, being the starting date (represented as serial number 1). Each subsequent day is represented by an incremental serial number.

For example:

- **=DATE(2023, 12, 31)** would generate the date December 31, 2023.

- **=DATE(2022, 6, 15)** would generate the date June 15, 2022.

Overview of how the DATE function assists in date manipulation and calculations.

The DATE function in Excel is a fundamental tool that greatly assists in date manipulation and various date-related calculations. Its functionality allows users to create and manage dates dynamically within formulas and functions. Here's an overview of how the DATE function aids in date manipulation and calculations:

1. **Date Creation:** The DATE function allows users to create date values by specifying the year, month, and day as separate arguments. This enables the dynamic generation of dates based on variable inputs.

2. **Dynamic Date Calculations:** Users can use the DATE function within formulas to perform various calculations involving dates, such as adding or subtracting days, months, or years to or from a specific date.

3. **Date Arithmetic:** It facilitates arithmetic operations with dates, allowing for the calculation of intervals between two dates in terms of days, months, or years.

84

4. **Date Comparison:** DATE function-generated dates can be used for comparisons between different dates, enabling the evaluation of date ranges, determining past or future dates, and conditional formatting based on date values.

5. **Data Analysis and Reporting:** Excel users utilize the DATE function to manage and analyze date-related data, such as tracking project timelines, calculating financial periods, generating reports based on specific date ranges, and forecasting future dates.

6. **Automation and Dynamic Worksheets:** When combined with other functions like TODAY or NOW, the DATE function aids in creating dynamic worksheets that automatically update date-related information based on the current date or specific date inputs.

7. **Date Formatting and Display:** DATE function-generated dates can be formatted to display in various date formats, enhancing the presentation of data according to specific requirements or regional conventions.

8. **Integration with Other Functions:** The DATE function integrates seamlessly with other Excel date and time functions, allowing for complex date-based calculations and manipulations within formulas and functions.

Dynamic Creation of Date in Excel

Using the DATE function in Excel allows for dynamic date creation by combining it with other functions to generate dates based on changing criteria or the current date. Here are a few examples:

1. Dynamic Creation of Today's Date:

To generate the current date dynamically, use the TODAY() function:

```
=TODAY()
```

This formula will return today's date whenever the worksheet is recalculated or opened on a new day

2. Creating a Date for the First Day of the Current Month:

To get the date for the first day of the current month, combine the DATE function with the YEAR and MONTH functions:

=DATE(YEAR(TODAY()), MONTH(TODAY()), 1)

This formula generates the date for the first day of the current month. For instance, if today's date is October 15, 2023, it will return October 1, 2023.

3. Calculating a Future Date:

To calculate a date, say, 30 days ahead of the current date:

=TODAY() + 30

4. Generating a Date Using Specific Inputs:

Suppose cells A1, A2, and A3 contain the year, month, and day values. You can use these values dynamically with the DATE function:

if today is November 20, 2023, this formula will give the date December 20, 2023, which is 30 days ahead.

=DATE(A1, A2, A3)

If A1 = 2024, A2 = 8 (for August), and A3 = 15, this formula will generate the date August 15, 2024.

Date Function for Data Analysis and Reporting in Excel

The DATE function in Excel is instrumental in data analysis and reporting, especially when dealing with date-related data. Here are a few examples demonstrating how the DATE function can be utilized for data analysis and reporting:

1. Age Calculation:

Suppose you have a list of birthdates in column A. You can use the DATE function with TODAY to calculate the age dynamically:

Assuming birthdates are in column A, to know the age , enter the formula below.

=YEAR(TODAY())-YEAR(A2)

Scenario

Suppose you want to obtain the ages of persons indicated in the table below, apply the formula mentioned earlier.

alibri   11   A A ≡ ≡ ≡

I U ▾ ⊞ ▾ ◇ ▾ A ▾ ≡ ≡ ≡ ⇐

Font

✓   ƒ✕   =YEAR(TODAY())-YEAR(D2)

C	D	E	F
	Date of Birth	Age	
	5/12/1978	45	
	10/22/2003	20	
	8/14/2010	13	
	4/16/1945	78	

2. Tracking Project Timelines:

For project management, the DATE function can be used to calculate deadlines and project durations. Suppose you have a project start date in cell A2 and a duration of 30 days:

=A2 + 30

3. Financial Reporting:

In financial reporting, the DATE function is helpful for managing reporting periods or forecasting. For example, to generate the first day of each month in a year:

=DATE(2023, ROW(), 1)

89

This formula, when dragged down in Excel, generates the first day of each month for the year 2023 using the ROW function.

4. Conditional Formatting Based on Dates:

Conditional formatting can be applied to highlight dates falling within a certain range. For instance, if you want to highlight overdue tasks with a red color, assuming the task deadlines are in column B:
=B2<TODAY()

Apply conditional formatting using this formula to cells in column B. It will highlight tasks with deadlines that have passed.

Scenario

Suppose you want to apply color red to those date below deadline given as 12/13/2023 for the project in the table below

Steps to Apply Conditional Formatting Based on Dates:

Step 1: Select the Range, select the range of cells containing the dates that you want to format based on specific conditions.

Step 2: Open Conditional Formatting Menu, navigate to the "Home" tab on the Excel ribbon, and click on "Conditional Formatting" in the toolbar.

Step 3: Choose New Rule

Select "New Rule" from the Conditional Formatting dropdown menu to open the New Formatting Rule dialog box.

Step 4: Define the Rule Based on Dates

Inside the New Formatting Rule dialog box:

For Example: Highlight Overdue Tasks

- **Select a Rule Type:** Choose "Use a formula to determine which cells to format."

- **Enter the Formula:** To highlight overdue dates (dates that have passed), use a formula like:

=A1<TODAY()

This formula assumes your dates are in cell A1. Adjust the cell reference as needed.

- **Set the Format:** Click on the "Format" button to set the formatting style for the cells meeting the condition (e.g., select a red fill color).

- **Apply the Rule:** Click "OK" to apply the rule and return to the main worksheet.

Step 5: Adjust Additional Rules (Optional)

You can add more rules for different conditions or modify the existing rule by repeating steps 3 and 4.

Step 6: Confirm Changes

Click "OK" to confirm and apply the conditional formatting rules.

Additional Tips:

- Use different date-related formulas within the conditional formatting rules (e.g., >TODAY() for future dates, =TODAY() for today's date).

- Experiment with various formatting styles, such as colors, fonts, or icon sets, to differentiate dates based on different conditions.

ISBLANK Function Explained

ISBLANK function in Excel is used to check if a cell is blank or empty. It returns TRUE if the cell is blank and FALSE if it contains any content (text, number, formula, space, or even an empty string "").

Syntax:

```
=ISBLANK(reference)
```

Argument

reference: The cell or range of cells you want to check for being blank or empty. Here are a few examples of how the ISBLANK function can be used:

1. Check if a single cell is blank

=ISBLANK(A1)   // This formula checks if cell A1 is blank.

2. Checking a Range of Cells for Blanks

=ISBLANK(A1:B10)   // This formula will return TRUE if any cell within the range A1:B10 is blank. If all cells in the range contain any content, it will return FALSE

3. Using ISBLANK with IF Function:

93

=IF(ISBLANK(A1), "Cell is blank", "Cell is not blank")   // This formula combines the ISBLANK function with the IF function to display a message based on whether cell A1 is blank or not.

Selected Practical Examples

1. Retrieving the First Non-Blank Values

In order to extract the first non-blank value in Excel from a range of cells, you can use the following formula.

```
=INDEX(B2:M2,1,MATCH(1,INDEX(1-ISBLANK(B2:M2),1,0),0))
```

Step 1: Click on an empty cell outside the table and enter the above formula.

	A	B	C	D	E	F	G	H	I
1					Sales				
2	Name	Jan	Feb	Mar	Apr	May	Jun	Jul	
3	Grey		$500	$200		$450		$500	
4	Joseph			$140		$200			
5	Bobby	$200	$600		$500	$450			
6	Clay		$245	$150	$300	$120			
7	Tony	$800	$320				$450		
8									
9		Grey	=INDEX(B3:H7,1,MATCH(1,INDEX(1-ISBLANK(B3:H7),1,0),))						
10		Joseph							
11		Bobby							
12		Clay							
13		Tony							
14									

Step 2: Click "Enter", then drag the cells downward to obtain values for other rows

A	B	C	D	E	F	G	H	I
1			Sales					
Name	Jan	Feb	Mar	Apr	May	Jun	Jul	
Grey		$500	$200		$450		$500	
Joseph			$140		$200			
Bobby	$200	$600		$500	$450			
Clay		$245	$150	$300	$120			
Tony	$800	$320				$450		
	Grey	500						
	Joseph	140						
	Bobby	200						
	Clay	245						
	Tony	800						

How the Formula Works

I. The ISBLANK function will return TRUE if a cell is blank and FALSE if the cell is not blank

II. Range B2:H2 will return FALSE, TRUE, TRUE, FALSE, TRUE, FALSE, TRUE

III. The TRUE and FALSE values are either a 1 or a 0 in an array formula. TRUE = 1 and FALSE = 0

IV. The 1-ISBLANK(B2:H7) will therefore return a 0 for a blank cell and a 1 for a non-blank cell. For example B2 will return a 0 because 1-1 = 0. Cell F2 will return a 1 because 1-0 = 1

V. NDEX(1-ISBLANK(B3:H7),1,0) will therefore return the array {0,1,1,0,1,0,1}

VI.   MATCH(1,INDEX(1-ISBLANK(B3:H7),1,0),0)   returns the first position of 1 in the array {0,1,1,0,1,0,1}In this array the first position of 1 is in position 2, i.e. Feb. If you break this formula down it will look like this MATCH(1, {0,1,1,0,1,0,1},0)"

VII. You know that the second column contains the first non-blank cell. You now need to return the value in this second column. This is where you use the INDEX function. To break this down the formula will be =INDEX(B3:H7,1,2)

VIII. This produces $500

2. Retrieving Unique Values in Excel

To extract unique values from a list in Excel, you can use several methods which includes: Advanced filter, Remove Duplicate Option and Macro. Here, I am going to employ the use of formulas

There are two versions of this method;

1. Using Formulas (for Excel versions supporting UNIQUE function):

   For Excel 365 or Excel 2019, you can use the UNIQUE function to extract unique values.

=UNIQUE(range, [by_col], [exactly_once]

- **range**: The range of cells or the array from which you want to extract unique values.

- **by_col** (optional): TRUE/FALSE. If TRUE, the function treats each column in the range as a separate data set.

- **exactly_once** (optional): TRUE/FALSE. If TRUE, it returns only values that appear exactly once.

  Example

  =UNIQUE(A1:A10)

2. Using Formulas (for older Excel versions without UNIQUE function):

   If your Excel version doesn't support the UNIQUE function, you can use formulas like **INDEX**, **MATCH**, and **COUNTIF** together to extract unique values.

Syntax:

```
=IFERROR(INDEX($A$1:$A$10, MATCH(0,
COUNTIF($B$1:B1, $A$1:$A$10), 0)), "")
```

Scenario

Consider the table below with a list of customers. Suppose you want to extract a list of unique names (i.e. without duplicates

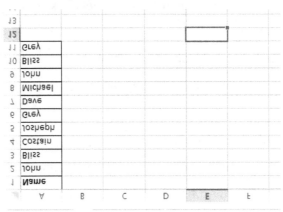

Copy the formula above and paste it in any empty cell. Hit **CTRL + SHIFT + ENTER.** If done correctly, Excel will rap the formula with curly braces {...}

To fill the column down, select the first cell with value and drag the edge down

	A	B	C	D	E	F	G	H	I	J	K
1	Name		unique names								
2	John		John								
3	Bliss		Bliss								
4	Costain		Costain								
5	Josheph		Josheph								
6	Grey		Grey								
7	Dave		Dave								
8	Michael		Michael								
9	John										
10	Bliss										
11	Grey										
12											

NOTE => suppose there are missing values or blank cells from the list you want to extract unique values, use the modified formula below:

```
=IFERROR(INDEX($A$2:$A$11,MATCH(0,IF(ISBLANK($A$2:$A$
11),1,COUNTIF($C$2:C2, $A$2:$A$11)), 0)),"")
```

How the formula works

1. **COUNTIF Function (COUNTIF($C$2:C2, $A$2:$A$11)):**

• **COUNTIF** counts the occurrences of each value in the range **$A$2:$A$11** that haven't been already extracted (up to the current row) in column B.

- **$C$1:C1** refers to the cells in column C from cell C1 up to the current row. As the formula is copied down, it expands to cover more rows, preventing already extracted values from being counted again.

2. **MATCH Function (MATCH(0, ..., 0)):**

- The **MATCH** function looks for the first occurrence of **0** (indicating a value that hasn't been extracted yet) within the array resulting from **COUNTIF**.

- The third argument **0** specifies an exact match.

3. **INDEX Function (INDEX($A$2:$A$11, ...)):**

- The **INDEX** function retrieves the unique values from the original list in range **$A$2:$A$11** based on the positions found by the **MATCH** function.

4. **IFERROR Function (IFERROR(..., "")):**

- The **IFERROR** function is used to handle any potential errors that may arise in the formula. If an error occurs (e.g., when the **MATCH** function can't find any more unique values), it returns an empty string "".

Points to Note:

✓ The range in the COUNTIF functions first argument starts in the row one above the formula. In this example it is cell C1

✓ You must press CTRL+SHIFT+ENTER to make the formula work

3. Retrieving an email address from a string of text

Extracting an email address from a text string in Excel can be done using various methods, especially if the email address follows a consistent pattern. These includes: using Text Function, Excel Flash Fill Feature and Regular Expression (with VBA). For simplicity and avoidance of Excel Version Support issue, I will use Text Function method.

If the email addresses follow a consistent pattern (e.g., they always contain "@" and "."), you can use a combination of text functions like **FIND, LEFT, RIGHT**, and **MID** to extract the email address.

For example, if the email addresses are separated by spaces and you want to extract the first email address from cell A1:

=IFERROR(TRIM(RIGHT(SUBSTITUTE(LEFT(A2,FIND(" ",A2&" ",FIND("@",A2))-1)," ",REPT("   ",LEN(A2))),LEN(A2))), "")
The given formula aims to manage diverse text formats by utilizing spaces as indicators and supposes that the email address comes before the space just preceding the "@" symbol. However, the reliability of this formula   could differ based on the distinct patterns and arrangements within your text information. It's crucial to test it across various text strings containing email addresses to verify precise extraction.

Scenario

Suppose you want to extract an email address from each   text string in the excel sheet below.

	A	B
1	**Text**	
2	Please contact me at john@gmail.com for details	
3	Reach me at ray2023@yahoo.comefor discussion	
4	Contact us at jamesshy@gmail.com officially	
5	Mail sent to call@gmail.com	
6		
7	Response should be sent to feedback@yahoo.com	
8		

Click on cell B2 and insert the formula given above, then press enter, and drag down to fill the remaining spaces

	A	B
1	**Text**	**Extracted Mail**
2	Please contact me at john@gmail.com for details	john@gmail.com
3	Reach me at ray2023@yahoo.comefor discussion	ray2023@yahoo.comefor
4	Contact us at jamesshy@gmail.com officially	jamesshy@gmail.com
5	Mail sent to call@gmail.com	call@gmail.com
6		
7	Response should be sent to feedback@yahoo.com	feedback@yahoo.com

How the Formula Works

1. **FIND("@", A2)**: This locates the position of the "@" symbol in the text in cell A2.

2. **FIND(" ", A2 & " ", FIND("@", A2))**: Finds the position of the space character before the "@" symbol by searching for a space from the "@" symbol's position.

3. **LEFT(A2, FIND(" ", A2 & " ", FIND("@", A2)) - 1)**: Extracts the substring from the start of the text in cell A2 until the space before the "@" symbol.

4. **SUBSTITUTE(..., " ", REPT(" ", LEN(A2)))**: Replaces all spaces in the extracted substring with spaces of the same length as the original text.

5. **RIGHT(..., LEN(A2))**: Extracts the right portion of the modified substring, which should be the email address.

6. **TRIM(...)**: Removes any leading or trailing spaces from the extracted email address.

7. **IFERROR(..., "")**: This part ensures that if any error occurs during the extraction (for instance, if there's no "@" symbol or the pattern doesn't match), it will return an empty string ("") instead of an error.

Note that cell A6 didn't contain an email address so the formula returned a blank value

Excel Tips, Tricks and Best Practices

Here are some Excel tips, tricks, and best practices that can help improve efficiency and productivity while working with Excel.

1. Minimize the Use of Volatile Functions:

Volatile functions like NOW(), TODAY(), and RAND() recalculate every time a change is made to the worksheet. Minimize their usage, especially in large datasets, to reduce unnecessary recalculations.

2. Use Relative References When Possible:

Utilize relative references (without $ symbols) within formulas. These references adjust automatically when copied or filled, reducing the need for manual adjustments and enhancing formula portability.

3. Replace Array Formulas with Regular Formulas:

Array formulas can slow down calculation speed, especially in extensive datasets. Where possible, replace array formulas with regular formulas to improve performance.

4. Limit the Use of Full Column/Row References:

Avoid using entire column or row references (e.g., A:A, 1:1) within formulas as they force Excel to calculate across the entire column/row, impacting performance. Instead, use specific ranges where needed.

5. Use Excel Tables for Data References:

Utilize Excel tables (Insert > Table) to create structured data ranges. Tables automatically expand/contract with data changes and improve formula efficiency due to structured references.

6. Employ Named Ranges:

Define named ranges (Formulas > Name Manager) to assign descriptive names to cell ranges. Named ranges make formulas more readable and maintainable, enhancing efficiency.

7. Limit Nested Functions:

Excessive nesting of functions (functions within functions) can make formulas complex and harder to manage.

Simplify formulas by breaking them into smaller, manageable parts or using helper columns.

8. Evaluate and Optimize Long Formulas:

Break down long formulas into smaller, intermediate steps using helper columns or cells. This not only enhances readability but also improves formula debugging and maintenance.

9. Use Calculation Options:

Modify Excel's calculation settings (Formulas > Calculation Options) to manual calculation when working with large datasets. This allows manual control of when calculations occur, reducing unnecessary recalculations.

10. Turn off Automatic Recalculation:

Temporarily turn off automatic calculation (Formulas > Calculation Options > Manual) when making extensive changes. This prevents Excel from recalculating after each modification, speeding up operations.

11. Monitor Workbook Size:

Large file sizes may slow down Excel's performance. Regularly remove unused data, clear formatting, and avoid unnecessary formulas or data to optimize file size.

12. Use Excel's Built-in Tools:

Leverage Excel's auditing tools (Formulas > Formula Auditing) like Evaluate Formula, Formula Auditing, and Trace Precedents/Dependents to identify and resolve formula errors or inefficiencies

Navigation and Selections

S/N	Excel Shortcuts	Function
1	Ctrl + Arrow Keys	Quickly navigate to the edges of your data in a column or row
3	Ctrl + Spacebar	Select an entire column
4	Shift + Spacebar	Select an entire row
5	Ctrl + Home	Move to the beginning of the worksheet
6	Ctrl + End	Go to the last cell in the worksheet

7	F4 Key	Repeat the last action or lock cell references in a formula
8	Alt + =	Quickly sum up values in the cells above or to the left of the active cell
9	Ctrl + Shift + L	Apply filters to your data quickly
10	Ctrl + E	Automatically fills your data when it detects a pattern in adjacent
11	Ctrl + Page Up/Page	Switch between worksheet tabs from left to right
12	Ctrl + ' (Apostrophe):	Copy the formula from the cell above
13	Ctrl + ~ (Tilde):	Display formulas instead of values

14	Ctrl + F2	Show the print preview of the active worksheet
16	Ctrl + A (Twice)	Select the entire worksheet. Pressing Ctrl + A second time selects the whole workbook
17	Ctrl + Shift + Arrow Keys	Extend your selection to the edge of the data in the direction of the arrow.
18	Shift + Click	Select multiple non-contiguous cells or ranges by holding down Shift while clicking on cells.

Excel Functions Quick Reference Guide

S/N	Excel Function	Used for
1	SUM	Calculates the sum of a range of numbers.
2	AVERAGE	Computes the average of a range of numbers
3	MAX/MIN	Finds the maximum/minimum value in a range
4	ROUND	Rounds a number to a specified number of decimal places
5	ABS	Returns the absolute value of a number
6	COUNT/COUNTA	Counts the number of cells that contain numbers/non-blank cells

7	COUNTIF/COUNTIFS	Counts cells that meet a specific criterion/criteria
8	SUMIF/SUMIFS	Adds cells based on a given criterion/criteria
9	AVERAGEIF/AVERAGEIFS	Calculates the average based on a given criterion/criteria
10	STDEV/STDEVP	Calculates the standard deviation of a sample/population
11	IF	Checks if a condition is met and returns one value if true and another if false
12	AND/OR	Evaluates multiple conditions and returns true if all/any conditions are met.

13	NOT	Reverses the logical value of its argument
14	IFERROR	Handles errors by specifying a value to return if an error occurs.
15	IFNA	Specifies a value to return if a formula results in a #N/A error
16	CONCATENATE	Specifies a value to return if a formula results in a #N/A error
17	LEFT/RIGHT/MID	Extracts characters from the left/right/middle of a text string
18	LEN	Returns the length (number of characters) in a text string
19	UPPER/LOWER/PROPER	Converts text to upper/lowercase or capitalizes the

		first letter of each word
20	TODAY/NOW	Returns the current date/time
21	DATE/DATEDIF	Constructs a date/returns the difference between two dates
22	YEAR/MONTH/DAY	Extracts the year/month/day from a date
23	EOMONTH	Returns the last day of the month
24	VLOOKUP/HLOOKUP	Searches for a value in a table and returns a corresponding value.
25	INDEX/MATCH	Retrieves a value at a specified location based on row/column position or specific criteria